Extreme Ownership

Jocko Willink & Leif Babin

Conversation Starters

By BookHabits

Please Note: This is an unofficial Conversation Starters guide. If you have not yet read the original work, you can purchase the original book here.

We hope you enjoy this complementary guide from BookHabits. Our mission is to aid readers and reading groups with quality, thought provoking material to in the discovery and discussions on some of today's favorite books.

Tips for Using Conversation Starters:

EVERY GOOD BOOK CONTAINS A WORLD FAR DEEPER THAN the surface of its pages. Questions herein are designed to bring us beneath the surface of the page and invite us into the world that lives on. These questions can be used to:

- Foster a deeper understanding of the book
- Promote an atmosphere of discussion for groups
- Assist in the study of the book, either individually or corporately
- Explore unseen realms of the book as never seen before

Table of Contents

Introducing *Extreme Ownership*

Extreme Ownership: How Navy SEALS Lead and Win is a book that teaches business leaders how to succeed by applying the principles and attitudes that enabled SEALs win in combat. It is written by SEAL officers Jocko Willink and Leif Babin who have much experience winning in the battlefields of Iraq and Afghanistan and who have trained the next generation of SEALs.

The authors believe that the leadership principles used in combat can be effectively used in business. The leadership style is the key factor that will determine an organization's success. Willink and Babin tell their stories as soldiers in the battlefield, describe how they succeeded in each battle situation, and cite the war principles that business people could adopt. Important lessons are highlighted. A leader should be capable of owning responsibility for the team, including mistakes and failures. The team members must be fully convinced of their group mission. Working with other teams increases likelihood of success and good results. Plans that are easy to understand are advantageous to the team. Ego should not get in the way of achieving the team's goals. Priorities have to be identified and be followed systematically. The mission should be clear. Include your superiors in the process of carrying out your mission, particularly when the process gets difficult. Be decisive. The book concludes by giving a summary of leadership qualities.

The book is composed of three parts: Winning the War Within, Laws of Combat, and Sustaining Victory. Each part has four chapters each of which represent a particular principle to be learned. Each chapter tells a battlefield story that highlights the principle in focus then explains how this principle is applied in business. There are 12 chapters in all.

The battle scenes are described in detail, giving readers a clear idea as to what truly happens in war. The stories are told in an engaging manner, complete with suspense and heart-stopping scenes. Military terms are used unsparingly, with footnotes that further explain what these terms mean. The jargon can discourage some readers, though others find it interesting. The stories are told in clear and simple language. The discussions on business leadership have an authoritative tone. Lessons and advice are stated directly and compellingly.

In the introduction, the authors explain the origins of the book, which is to document the leadership principles used by Navy SEALS in Iraq and Afghanistan, wars that resulted from the September 11, 2001 terrorist attacks in the US. It is meant for future generation of SEALS to remind them of how the wars were fought and to learn from them. They also wrote the book as lessons in leadership for people beyond the battlefield, particularly those in organizations and corporations. The theme centers on winning the battle, both on the field and in business setting. Good leadership as a means to winning the war is communicated well through the examples of leaders in the battlefield. The authors are able to define the qualities of a good leader and what it takes for the team to win. Conversations with business leaders are told to further stress the importance of the principles. The action-filled stories in the battlefield are entertaining and provide interesting information to readers. Though some consider it unpleasant because of the savage war scenes, the military talk, and the tone of authority, the book's teachings are nevertheless useful to people in leadership positions.

Though the authors say that it is not a memoir, the stories told from the first-person perspective read like it is partly memoir. The book is an unlikely combination of business leadership strategy and combat stories. While the war stories were engaging, the accounts of conversations with CEOs and business leaders appear contrived and therefore not believable according to readers. Photographs placed between chapters show war scenes and sites of action, war ruins, maps, and the soldiers in action. These give a visceral feeling about the war stories, enabling readers to understand and feel deeper about the war. Readers say that the authors start to become repetitive as the book nears the end. The emphasis on winning is also off putting for some readers. Many readers expressed fascination with the war stories. The last part of the book rounds up what has been explained in the previous chapters, and explores the seemingly contradictory qualities of a leader. They also say being a leader is the most rewarding and gratifying experience one can ever have, despite all the difficult challenges it presents and the lack of assurance that success will happen.

This *New York Times* bestseller revolutionizes the way businesses are managed, with an eye on winning the game.

Discussion Questions

"Get Ready to Enter a New World"

Tip: Begin with questions dealing with broader issues to ensure ample time for quality discussions. Read through all discussion questions before engaging.

~~~

question 1

Extreme Ownership is a book that teaches business people how to succeed. What is the book's idea of succeeding? Is it comparable to the business setting?

~~~

~~~

question 2

The authors believe that the leadership principles used in combat can be effectively used in business. What are the similarities between field combat and business?

~~~

~~~

question 3

According to the authors, the leadership style is the key factor that will determine an organization's success. What kind of leaders are Willink and Babin? Why are they qualified to write the book?

~~~

~~~

question 4

Willink and Babin fill the book with their stories as soldiers in the battlefield. Which of the stories do you like best? Why?

~~~

~~~

question 5

A leader should be capable of owning responsibility for the team, including mistakes and failures. How do you feel about this principle? Have you been in a situation that involved taking responsibility?

~~~

~~~

question 6

Another important principle is that the team members must be fully convinced of their group mission. How does this affect the group's success or failure?

~~~

~~~

question 7

The book is well-organized and well-structured. How do the authors organize their ideas? How is each chapter organized?

~~~

~~~

question 8

The battle scenes are engaging. What makes them entertaining and worth listening to? How do the authors tell them?

~~~

~~~

question 9

Military terms are used unsparingly, with footnotes that explain what these terms mean. How do you feel about the use of military terms? Do the authors help you understand them?

~~~

~~~

question 10

The discussions on business leadership have an authoritative tone. Is the tone appropriate to the theme of the book? Why? Why not?

~~~

~~~

question 11

Though the authors say that it is not a memoir, the stories told from the first-person perspective read like it is partly memoir. Would you say it is partly memoir? Why? Why not?

~~~

~~~

question 12

Photographs placed between chapters show war scenes and sites of action, war ruins, maps, and the soldiers in action. How do the photos affect the overall content of the book?

~~~

~~~

question 13

The last part of the book rounds up what has been explained in the previous chapters, and gives an encouraging reminder for leaders. What about being a leader that they want readers to remember?

~~~

~~~

question 14

The book is an unlikely combination of business strategy and combat stories. Do you think it's a good combination? Why? Why not?

~~~

~~~

question 15

The authors include accounts of conversations with CEOs and business leaders. How are these conversations written? Do you like the way they were written?

~~~

~~~

question 16

Entrepreneur and philanthropist Amy Brandt Schumacher thinks *Extreme Ownership* will "dramatically improve" leaders from all backgrounds. Do you agree with her? Will you recommend this book to your leader friends? Why? Why not?

~~~

~~~

question 17

A Goodreads review says the book becomes repetitive towards the end. Have you noticed where it becomes repetitive? How could this have been avoided by the authors?

~~~

~~~

question 18

An Amazon review says the book lacks emotion, is cold, and is restrained. Why do you think the reviewers says this? Do you agree with these comments?

~~~

~~~

question 19

Netscape co-founder Marc Andreessen says the book is one of the best leadership books he has read. Coming from a leader in the software industry, how does this affect your impression of the book?

~~~

~~~

question 20

The book is written by Willink who has another *New York Times* bestselling book, *Discipline Equals Freedom*. How do you think the bestseller *Extreme Ownership* will be accepted by Willink's readers who bought his other book? Is it bestselling because of Willink's previous influence?

~~~

Introducing the Author

Jocko Willink and Leif Babin are founders of Echelon Front, a company that offers expert advice for complex problems, based on the founders' real-life experience dealing with challenging situations. Willink and Babin serve as executive coaches, instructors and speakers on leadership topics and issues. Their clients include individuals and organizations from a broad range of disciplines and industries. Both are retired Navy SEAL officers, Willink having spent 20 years in service while Babin did 13 years. Willink led the SEAL's Task Unit Bruiser which became the most recognized unit for its role in fighting the terrorist group Al-Qaeda in Iraq in 2006. He led the training for SEAL Teams in the West Coast where he helped develop the leadership curriculum and personally mentored SEAL leaders who went on to perform successfully in the battlefield. He has authored two other books, *Way of the Warrior* and his other *New York Times* bestselling title, *Discipline Equals Freedom*.

Babin was platoon commander of the SEAL's Task Unit Bruiser in the Iraq war, and later on, a leadership instructor for SEAL officers. His awards include the Silver Star, Bronze Stars, and the Purple Heart. He has given talks on leadership, foreign policy and military strategy, appearing on TV and radio programs. He has written for the *Wall Street*

Journal. Babin has expressed strong opinions on various issues affecting American society. On gun control, he believes that less control on guns rather than a tighter one would be better for preventing crime. The presence of tight gun laws will discourage attackers from openly attacking schools, universities, theaters and similar areas. He thinks there is political value in sharing to the public the heroic military exploits that rescued prisoners of war but this is endangering the troops and future rescue missions. He is married to Fox News Channel anchor Jeena Lee.

In their book, Willink and Babin stress that a good leader knows how to lead but also knows how to be a follower. There are times when subordinates have better knowledge of a particular situation and the leaders should not let ego rule for the sake of the mission's success. The authors also cite situations during their battle stint in Ramadi, Iraq where they knew that a leader must be courageous but knows when to pull back. An example is a particular situation involving a planned attack which had to be delayed in order to clarify every detail of the plan. Willink as the unit's leader said it was frustrating to other units they worked with but he wanted to prevent any mistakes that could result to the death of American soldiers. Another quality of a good leader is being able to express his feelings of anger or frustration but should not lose his temper to the point of losing the respect of his subordinates. He can be confident but not to the point of being complacent and arrogant. These qualities seem to be contradictory but a leader can learn to balance such forces and be effective.

Fireside Questions

"What would you do?"

Tip: These questions can be a fun exercise as it spurs creativity among the readers by allowing alternate scene endings and "if this was you" questions.

~~~

question 21

Jocko Willink and Leif Babin are founders of Echelon Front. What does the company do and who are their clients?

~~~

~~~

question 22

Both are retired Navy SEAL officers. How long have they served as SEALs? How would you describe their military careers?

~~~

~~~

question 23

Willink has authored two other books, *Way of the Warrior* and his other *New York Times* bestselling title, *Discipline Equals Freedom*. In what way are these two books similar or related to *Extreme Ownership*?

~~~

~~~

question 24

Babin has given talks on leadership topics including areas in foreign policy and military strategy, appearing on TV and radio programs. What are some of his opinions that you have read or heard of? Do you agree with his views on gun control?

~~~

~~~

question 25

The authors explain leadership qualities that seem to be contradictory . What are some of these contradictory qualities and how can they be reconciled in a leader?

~~~

~~~

question 26

SEAL officers Jocko Willink and Leif Babin have much experience winning in the battlefields of Iraq and Afghanistan and who now train the next generation of SEALs.

If you are given the choice to train under these two leaders, how would you feel? Would you want them as mentors or would you choose others of a different perspective? Why?

~~~

~~~

question 27

Each chapter tells a battlefield story that highlights the principle in focus then explains how this principle is applied in business. If you are the editor would you suggest a different way of organizing the book? If yes, how would you want the chapters written?

~~~

~~~

question 28

The military jargon can discourage some readers, though others find it interesting. If you are the editor, would you retain the military terms? How would you go about telling their stories without using too much military language?

~~~

~~~

question 29

While the war stories were engaging, the accounts of conversations with CEOs and business leaders appear contrived and therefore not believable according to readers. If you are given the chance to rewrite the book for them, how would you change the part on teaching business leaders about the leadership principles. Will you continue to use and quote conversations?

~~~

~~~

question 30

The photos give a visceral feeling about the war stories, enabling readers to understand and feel deeper about the war. If given the chance to add changes to the book, what will you do with the photos? Will you add more or change the layout for a different effect?

~~~

Quiz Questions

"Ready to Announce the Winners?"

Tip: Create a leaderboard and track scores to see who gets the most correct answers. Winners required. Prizes optional.

~~~

quiz question 1

According to the authors, a leader should be capable of owning __________ for the team, including mistakes and failures.

~~~

~~~

quiz question 2

Though the authors say that the book is not a __________, the stories told from the first-person perspective read like it is like partly one.

~~~

~~~

quiz question 3

Reviewers say the book revolutionizes the way ____________ are managed, with an eye on winning the game.

~~~

~~~

quiz question 4

True or False: The last part of the book rounds up what has been explained in the previous chapters, and explores the seemingly contradictory qualities of a leader.

~~~

~~~

quiz question 5

True or False: The book is a combination of business leadership strategy and combat stories.

~~~

~~~

quiz question 6

True or False: The theme centers on proving to subordinates that leadership is about knowing more than the others.

~~~

~~~

quiz question 7

True or False: In the introduction, the authors explain the origins of the book, which is to document the leadership principles used by Navy SEALS.

~~~

~~~

quiz question 8

Jocko Willink and Leif Babin are founders of __________, a company that offers expert advice for complex problems, based on the founders' real-life experience dealing with challenging situations.

~~~

~~~

quiz question 9

True or False: Willink and Babin stress that a good leader knows how to lead but also knows how to be a follower.

~~~

~~~

quiz question 10

________ has given talks on leadership, foreign policy and military strategy, appearing on TV and radio programs. He has written for the *Wall Street Journal*.

~~~

~~~

quiz question 11

True or False: Both authors are retired Navy SEAL officers, Willink having spent 20 years in service while Babin did 13 years.

~~~

~~~

quiz question 12

True or False: Willink led the SEAL's Task Unit Bruiser which became the most recognized unit for its role in fighting the terrorist group Al-Qaeda in Iraq.

~~~

Quiz Answers

1. responsibility
2. memoir
3. businesses
4. True
5. True
6. False
7. True
8. Echelon Front
9. True
10. Leif Babin
11. True
12. True

Ways to Continue Your Reading

EVERY month, our team runs through a wide selection of books to pick the best titles for readers and reading groups, and promotes these titles to our thousands of readers – sometimes with free downloads, sale dates, and additional brochures.

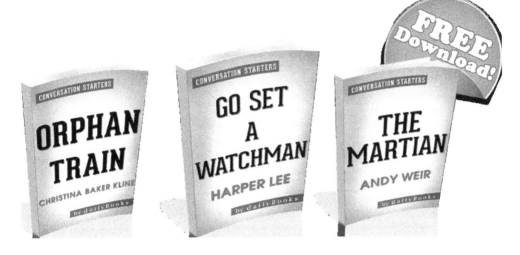

On the Next Page...

If you found this book helpful to your discussions and rate it a 4 or 5, please write us a review on the next page.

Any length would be fine but we'd appreciate hearing you more! We'd be very encouraged.

Till next time,

BookHabits

"Loving Books is Actually a Habit"

CPSIA information can be obtained
at www.ICGtesting.com
Printed in the USA
LVHW111740210119
604677LV00001B/42/P